New England
Patriots
TRIVIA CHALLENGE

SOURCEBOOKS, INC.®
NAPERVILLE, ILLINOIS

Published by Sourcebooks, Inc.
P.O. Box 4410, Naperville, Illinois 60567-4410
(630) 961-3900
Fax: (630) 961-2168
www.sourcebooks.com

Printed and bound in Canada
WC 10 9 8 7 6 5 4 3

Since joining the National Football League in 1970, the New England Patriots have been one of the most exciting franchises in the sport. While the early days of the franchise tested its fan's loyalty, the dynasty the team has built in the twenty-first century has given them all reason to believe. Players like John Hannah, Mike Haynes, and Andre Tippett built the foundation, then legendary coach Bill Belichick used players like Tom Brady, Tedy Bruschi, and Richard Seymour to cement the franchise's place in NFL history.

These 200 questions should test your knowledge of both coaches and athletes, from all-time passing records to once-in-a-lifetime game-winning plays, from the quirky comments coaches have made to the game-day traditions that cooked up the crowd during cold games at Gillette Stadium. If you are both a passionate fan and a stat geek, you should be able to get to the last page without clicking on your browser or calling your fellow fan. The questions and topics are designed with all levels of difficulty, from the biggest names to the obscure and bizarre. Get even half the answers right, and you can rightfully call yourself a Pats fan. Any less than that, and Coach Belichick will want to see you in his office.

FRANCHISE HISTORY

1. **What was the team's original name?**
   a. Boston Braves
   b. Massachusetts Patriots
   c. Boston Patriots
   d. Bay State Patriots

2. **Who led the group of Boston businessmen that was awarded the AFL's eighth and final franchise?**
   a. Mike Holovak
   b. Billy Sullivan
   c. Ed McKeever
   d. Phil Bissell

3. **What year did the Patriots take the field for the first time?**
   a. 1950
   b. 1955
   c. 1959
   d. 1960

4. **Who did the Patriots play in their first regular season game?**
   a. Denver Broncos
   b. Los Angeles Chargers
   c. Dallas Texans
   d. Buffalo Bills

5. Who did the Patriots defeat, 28-24, for their first win?

a. Denver Broncos
b. Oakland Raiders
c. Houston Oilers
d. New York Titans

6. What was the Patriots' record during their inaugural season?

a. 3-11
b. 5-9
c. 7-7
d. 8-5-1

7. Who scored the first regular season points for the Patriots?

a. Jim Colclough
b. Butch Songin
c. Gino Cappelletti
d. Dick Christy

8. Who scored the first regular season touchdown for the Patriots?

a. Jim Colclough
b. Dick Christy
c. Alan Miller
d. Ron Burton

9. What season saw the team's first playoff appearance?

a. 1961
b. 1963
c. 1967
d. 1969

10. **Who defeated the Patriots in their only AFL Championship game?**

    a. Buffalo Bills
    b. New York Jets
    c. Dallas Texans
    d. San Diego Chargers

11. **As of 2009, how many Super Bowls have the Patriots played in?**

    a. 4
    b. 5
    c. 6
    d. 7

12. **What division do the Patriots play in?**

    a. AFC North
    b. NFC North
    c. AFC East
    d. NFC East

13. **When did the Patriots win their first division title?**

    a. 1977
    b. 1963
    c. 1979
    d. 1980

14. **Which of the following teams does NOT play in a division with the Patriots?**

    a. Baltimore Ravens
    b. Buffalo Bills
    c. New York Jets
    d. Miami Dolphins

15. **What is the name of the Patriots' mascot?**

    a. Patriot Pete
    b. Pat Patriot
    c. Boston Bob
    d. Paul Revere

16. What is the name of the group of ten men who fire their muskets after every Patriots score?

a. The Revolutionaries
b. The Touchdown Patrol
c. The End-Zone Militia
d. The Minutemen

COACHES

17. Who was the first head coach of the Patriots?

a. Billy Sullivan
b. Mike Holovak
c. Lou Saban
d. Clive Rush

18. Who was the first Patriot coach to win Coach of the Year honors?

a. Mike Holovak
b. Chuck Fairbanks
c. Bill Parcells
d. Bill Belichick

19. Who has the longest tenure as head coach of the Patriots?

a. Chuck Fairbanks
b. Mike Holovak
c. Bill Parcells
d. Bill Belichick

20. How many times did the Patriots make the playoffs under Bill Parcells?

a. 1
b. 2
c. 3
d. 0

21. **Who did NOT serve as head coach during the 1978 season?**

    a. Chuck Fairbanks
    b. John Mazur
    c. Hank Bullough
    d. Ron Erhardt

22. **Which coach did NOT lead the Patriots to the Super Bowl?**

    a. Ron Meyer
    b. Bill Parcells
    c. Bill Belichick
    d. Raymond Berry

23. **Who did Bill Parcells replace as Patriots coach?**

    a. Rod Rust
    b. Pete Carroll
    c. Dick MacPherson
    d. Raymond Berry

24. **Which head coach famously said of the Patriots, "If they want you to cook the dinner, at least they ought to let you shop for some of the groceries"?**

    a. Pete Carroll
    b. Bill Parcells
    c. Bill Belichick
    d. Dick MacPherson

25. **With what other team did Bill Belichick serve as a head coach from 1991–95?**

    a. New York Giants
    b. New York Jets
    c. Baltimore Ravens
    d. Cleveland Browns

26. **What organization hired Belichick as head coach, only to have him resign a day later?**

    a. New York Giants
    b. New York Jets
    c. Miami Dolphins
    d. Minnesota Vikings

27. **What is Bill Belichick most famous for wearing on the sideline?**

    a. coat and tie
    b. warm-up suit
    c. hooded sweatshirt
    d. sunglasses

28. **Where did Bill Belichick attend college?**

    a. University of Connecticut
    b. Brown University
    c. Wesleyan University
    d. University of Pittsburgh

29. **Which team gave Bill Belichick his first NFL coaching job in 1975?**

    a. New York Giants
    b. Baltimore Colts
    c. Detroit Lions
    d. Denver Broncos

30. **Which of the following NCAA head coaches is not a member of Bill Belichick's "coaching tree"?**

    a. Nick Saban
    b. Kirk Ferentz
    c. Charlie Weis
    d. Pete Carroll

HOME FIELD ADVANTAGE

31. **What is the name of the Patriots' home field?**

    a. Patriots Field
    b. Gillette Stadium
    c. Schick Stadium
    d. Fenway Park

32. **When did the Patriots move in to their current stadium?**

    a. 2000
    b. 2001
    c. 2002
    d. 2003

33. **Where did the Patriots play before moving into Gillette Stadium?**

    a. Foxboro Stadium
    b. Patriot Stadium
    c. H.H.H. Metrodome
    d. Belichick Park

34. **Which of these was NOT a name used for the building the Patriots played from 1971–2001?**

    a. Foxboro Stadium
    b. Sullivan Stadium
    c. Schaefer Stadium
    d. Boston Stadium

35. **What was the name of the first stadium the Patriots played in?**

   a. Fenway Park
   b. Nickerson Field
   c. Foxboro Stadium
   d. Boston Park

36. **Who else plays games at Gillette Stadium?**

   a. Boston Red Sox
   b. Boston Bruins
   c. New England Revolution
   d. Boston College

37. **What was NOT a stadium the Patriots called home for at least one season?**

   a. Fonway Park
   b. Harvard Stadium
   c. Alumni Stadium
   d. Terrier Field

38. **What was Gillette Stadium originally going to be called?**

   a. Patriots Stadium
   b. Yahoo! Stadium
   c. CGMI Stadium
   d. Google Stadium

39. **As of the 2009 season, what is the capacity of Gillette Stadium?**

   a. 68,756
   b. 69,914
   c. 71,222
   d. 75,438

40. **In what city is Gillette Stadium located?**

   a. Boston, MA
   b. Foxborough, MA
   c. Cambridge, MA
   d. Quincy, MA

AWARDS AND HONORS

41. As of 2009, how many players who spent the majority of their careers with the Patriots are in the Pro Football Hall of Fame?

a. 3
b. 4
c. 5
d. 6

42. Which of these players are NOT enshrined in the Pro Football Hall of Fame?

a. Steve Nelson
b. Nick Buoniconti
c. John Hannah
d. Andre Tippett

43. Who became the first Patriot enshrined in the Pro Football Hall of Fame in 1991?

a. Mike Haynes
b. Nick Buoniconti
c. John Hannah
d. Andre Tippett

44. Which Patriot was enshrined in the Pro Football Hall of Fame in 2008?

a. Mike Haynes
b. Nick Buoniconti
c. John Hannah
d. Andre Tippett

45. How many numbers have the Patriots retired?

a. 4
b. 6
c. 7
d. 10

46. Which of these players does NOT have his number retired by the Patriots?

a. Nick Buoniconti - #85
b. Gino Capelletti - #20
c. Bruce Armstrong - #78
d. Bob Dee - #89

47. Who won AFL MVP honors for the Patriots in 1963?

a. Babe Parilli
b. Larry Garron
c. Larry Eisenhauer
d. Gino Capelletti

48. Who is the only Patriot to win NFL MVP and Offensive Player of the Year in the same season?

a. Randy Moss
b. Tom Brady
c. Curtis Martin
d. Jim Nance

49. Which coach never won a Coach of the Year award with the Patriots?

a. Raymond Berry
b. Chuck Fairbanks
c. Mike Holovak
d. Pete Carroll

50. Which Patriot was named Comeback Player of the Year in 2005?

a. Ben Watson
b. Tom Brady
c. Tedy Bruschi
d. Deion Branch

51. **Who holds the Patriot record with nine Pro Bowl appearances?**

    a. Jon Morris
    b. Tom Brady
    c. John Hannah
    d. Bruce Armstrong

52. **John Hannah holds the team record by being named First Team All-Pro seven times. Who is second?**

    a. Tom Brady
    b. Andre Tippett
    c. Richard Seymour
    d. Nick Buoniconti

53. **Since the 1970 NFL-AFL merger, what is the Patriots' record for Pro-Bowlers in a season?**

    a. 6
    b. 7
    c. 8
    d. 9

54. **Which former Patriot is the namesake for the award given to the College Football Special Teams Player of the Year?**

    a. Mosi Tatupu
    b. Dave Meggett
    c. Irving Fryar
    d. Troy Brown

1985 SEASON

55. **Who did the Patriots play in Super Bowl XX?**

a. Chicago Bears
b. Green Bay Packers
c. Philadelphia Eagles
d. San Francisco 49ers

56. **Which of the following teams did the Patriots NOT defeat during their playoff run to the Super Bowl?**

a. New York Jets
b. Los Angeles Raiders
c. Houston Oilers
d. Miami Dolphins

57. **Who recovered a Walter Payton fumble on the game's second play?**

a. Andre Tippett
b. Raymond Clayborn
c. Steve Nelson
d. Larry McGrew

58. **How many rushing yards did the Patriots record in Super Bowl XX?**

a. 7
b. 17
c. 27
d. 37

59. Who did NOT represent the Patriots in the Pro Bowl following the 1985 season?

a. Andre Tippett
b. Craig James
c. Tony Eason
d. Steve Nelson

1996 SEASON

60. **Who did the Patriots play in Super Bowl XXXI?**

    a. Chicago Bears
    b. Green Bay Packers
    c. New York Giants
    d. Philadelphia Eagles

61. **Where was Super Bowl XXXI held?**

    a. Phoenix, AZ
    b. Minneapolis, MN
    c. Houston, TX
    d. New Orleans, LA

62. **What was the Patriots' regular season record in 1996?**

    a. 10-6
    b. 11-5
    c. 12-4
    d. 13-3

63. **What weather phenomenon was prevalent in the Patriots' 28-3 divisional playoff win against the Pittsburgh Steelers?**

    a. snow
    b. rain
    c. fog
    d. wind

64. **Who did NOT represent the Patriots in the Pro Bowl following the 1996 season?**

    a. Drew Bledsoe
    b. Terry Glenn
    c. Curtis Martin
    d. Dave Meggett

2001 SEASON

65. What was the Patriots' regular season record in 2001?

a. 14-2
b. 13-3
c. 12-4
d. 11-5

66. Which team did NOT defeat the Patriots in the 2001 regular season?

a. New York Jets
b. San Diego Chargers
c. Cincinnati Bengals
d. Miami Dolphins

67. When did starting quarterback Drew Bledsoe sustain an injury, opening the door for Tom Brady?

a. training camp
b. first preseason game
c. week two
d. week four

68. How many regular season passes had Tom Brady thrown before taking over for Bledsoe?

a. 3
b. 6
c. 9
d. 0

69. Who did the Patriots defeat in Super Bowl XXXVI for their first championship?

a. Chicago Bears
b. St. Louis Rams
c. Green Bay Packers
d. Carolina Panthers

70. Where was Super Bowl XXXVI played?

a. Tampa, FL
b. Miami, FL
c. Dallas, TX
d. New Orleans, LA

71. Who sang the National Anthem?

a. Whitney Houston
b. Fergie
c. Mariah Carey
d. Beyonce Knowles

72. What was the score of the game?

a. 20-17
b. 32-29
c. 24-21
d. 17-14

73. How long was Adam Vinatieri's game-winning field goal?

a. 32-yards
b. 39-yards
c. 44-yards
d. 48-yards

74. How much time was on the clock when the Patriots lined up for Vinatieri's game winner?

a. 10 seconds
b. 7 seconds
c. 4 seconds
d. 1 second

75. Who was named Super Bowl XXXVI MVP??

a. Tom Brady
b. Ty Law
c. Adam Vinatieri
d. David Patten

76. Who had a 97-yard fumble recovery touchdown called back due to holding?

a. Mike Vrabel
b. Richard Seymour
c. Otis Smith
d. Tebucky Jones

77. Who was called for holding on the play?

a. Bobby Hamilton
b. Willie McGinest
c. Brandon Mitcholl
d. Ty Law

78. Which Ram scored a 26-yard touchdown to tie the game with 1:30 left?

a. Isaac Bruce
b. Az-Zahir Hakim
c. Marshall Faulk
d. Ricky Proehl

79. Who did NOT intercept a pass or recover a fumble for the Patriots in Super Bowl XXXVI?

a. Lawyer Milloy
b. Ty Law
c. Otis Smith
d. Terrell Buckley

80. Who caught an 8-yard touchdown pass with just 31 seconds left in the first half to extend the Patriots' lead to 14-3?

a. Troy Brown
b. David Patten
c. Jermaine Wiggins
d. J. R. Redmond

81. **How many yards did Tom Brady pass for in Super Bowl XXXVI?**

    a. 145
    b. 195
    c. 215
    d. 235

82. **How many turnovers did the Patriots' offense commit?**

    a. 1
    b. 2
    c. 3
    d. 0

83. **Who was the game's leading rusher with 92 yards?**

    a. Marshall Faulk
    b. Antowain Smith
    c. Kevin Faulk
    d. Trung Canidate

84. **Who was the game's leading receiver with 90 yards?**

    a. Troy Brown
    b. David Patten
    c. Isaac Bruce
    d. Az-Zahir Hakim

85. **What was the Patriots' third down conversion rate during Super Bowl XXXVI?**

    a. 2-11
    b. 5-10
    c. 7-12
    d. 10-13

86. **When the Patriots and Rams met during the 2001 regular season, what was the outcome?**

    a. Rams won 38-10
    b. Rams won 24-17
    c. Patriots won 20-17
    d. Patriots won 24-21

2003 SEASON

87. What was the Patriots' record during the 2003 regular season?

  a. 15-1
  b. 14-2
  c. 13-3
  d. 12-4

88. Which of the following teams defeated the Patriots on opening day of the 2003 season?

  a. Buffalo Bills
  b. New York Jets
  c. Denver Broncos
  d. Jacksonville Jaguars

89. What was the score of that opening day loss?

  a. 28-14
  b. 10-3
  c. 17-12
  d. 31-0

90. How many consecutive games did the Patriots win to close out the regular season?

  a. 8
  b. 9
  c. 11
  d. 12

91. **Who was the Patriots leading receiver with 57 receptions for 803 yards during the 2003 season?**

   a. Troy Brown
   b. Deion Branch
   c. David Patten
   d. David Givens

92. **Who intercepted Indianapolis Colts' quarterback Peyton Manning three times in the 2003 AFC Championship game?**

   a. Tyrone Poole
   b. Rodney Harrison
   c. Ty Law
   d. Eugene Wilson

93. **Who did the Patriots defeat in Super Bowl XXXVIII?**

   a. Green Bay Packers
   b. New York Giants
   c. Philadelphia Eagles
   d. Carolina Panthers

94. **Where was Super Bowl XXXVIII played?**

   a. New Orleans, LA
   b. Houston, TX
   c. Jacksonville, FL
   d. Miami, FL

95. **What was the score of the game?**

   a. 17-10
   b. 20-17
   c. 32-29
   d. 21-10

96. **How long was Adam Vinatieri's game-winning field goal?**

   a. 36 yards
   b. 39 yards
   c. 41 yards
   d. 44 yards

97. **How much time was left after Vinatieri hit the game-winning field goal?**

   a. 10 seconds
   b. 7 seconds
   c. 4 seconds
   d. 1 second

98. **How much time was on the clock when the Patriots started their final drive?**

   a. 2:00
   b. 1:31
   c. 1:08
   d. 0:52

99. **Who caught the 17-yard pass that set up Vinatieri's game-winning field goal?**

   a. Troy Brown
   b: Deion Branch
   c. David Givens
   d. Daniel Graham

100. **Who was named Super Bowl XXXVIII MVP?**

   a. Tom Brady
   b. Adam Vinatieri
   c. David Givens
   d. Antowain Smith

101. **Who scored the first touchdown of Super Bowl XXXVIII?**
   a. David Givens
   b. Deion Branch
   c. Antowain Smith
   d. Kevin Faulk

102. **How many yards did Tom Brady throw for in the game?**
   a. 274
   b. 298
   c. 321
   d. 354

103. **Who did Tom Brady NOT throw a touchdown pass to?**
   a. Deion Branch
   b. David Givens
   c. Daniel Graham
   d. Mike Vrabel

104. **Tom Brady set a Super Bowl record with how many completions?**
   a. 28
   b. 32
   c. 35
   d. 37

105. **How many points did the two teams combine for in the fourth quarter, setting a Super Bowl record?**
   a. 28
   b. 30
   c. 32
   d. 37

106. **Who scored on a game-high 85-yard reception for Carolina?**
   a. Steve Smith
   b. Muhsin Muhammad
   c. Ricky Proehl
   d. DeShaun Foster

107. **Who was the game's leading rusher with 83 yards?**
   a. Antowain Smith
   b. Kevin Faulk
   c. Stephen Davis
   d. DeShaun Foster

108. **Who was the game's leading receiver with 143 yards?**
   a. David Givens
   b. Deion Branch
   c. Steve Smith
   d. Muhsin Muhammad

109. **Who was the referee in Super Bowl XXXVIII?**
   a. Jeff Rice
   b. Ben Montgomery
   c. Ed Hochuli
   d. Mark Hittner

110. **Who performed the halftime show at Super Bowl XXXVIII?**
   a. Aerosmith
   b. U2
   c. The Rolling Stones
   d. Janet Jackson

2004 SEASON

111. What was the Patriots' record during the 2004 regular season?

a. 16-0
b. 15-1
c. 14-2
d. 13-3

112. After winning their first six regular season games, the Patriots set an NFL record with how many consecutive regular season wins?

a. 16
b. 18
c. 20
d. 22

113. Who defeated the Patriots, 34-20, to end their record streak?

a. San Diego Chargers
b. New York Giants
c. Pittsburgh Steelers
d. Minnesota Vikings

114. Which team broke that record with 21 consecutive regular season wins from 2006-08?

a. Green Bay Packers
b. New York Giants
c. Philadelphia Eagles
d. New England Patriots

115. Who set a franchise record with 1,635 rushing yards in 2004?

a. Antowain Smith
b. Corey Dillon
c. Kevin Faulk
d. Cedric Cobbs

116. Which wide receiver was forced to play cornerback during part of the 2004 season due to multiple injuries in the secondary?

a. David Patten
b. David Givens
c. Troy Brown
d. Deion Branch

117. Who did the Patriots defeat in Super Bowl XXXIX?

a. Philadelphia Eagles
b. New York Giants
c. St. Louis Rams
d. Minnesota Vikings

118. What was the score of Super Bowl XXXIX?

a. 17-14
b. 32-28
c. 24-21
d. 21-17

119. Where was Super Bowl XXXIX played?

a. Houston, TX
b. Jacksonville, FL
c. Detroit, MI
d. New Orleans, LA

120. Who was named Super Bowl XXXIX MVP?

a. Tom Brady
b. Corey Dillon
c. Mike Vrabel
d. Deion Branch

121. **Deion Branch tied a Super Bowl record with how many receptions?**

    a. 10
    b. 11
    c. 12
    d. 13

122. **Who scored the first touchdown in Super Bowl XXXIX?**

    a. Corey Dillon
    b. David Givens
    c. L. J. Smith
    d. Brian Westbrook

123. **Who rushed for a game-high 75 yards in Super Bowl XXXIX?**

    a. Corey Dillon
    b. Kevin Faulk
    c. Brian Westbrook
    d. Correll Buckhalter

124. **Who did NOT score a touchdown for the Patriots in Super Bowl XXXIX?**

    a. David Givens
    b. Deion Branch
    c. Corey Dillon
    d. Mike Vrabel

125. **How many turnovers did the Patriots' defense force in Super Bowl XXXIX?**

    a. 2
    b. 3
    c. 4
    d. 0

126. **Who intercepted a Donovan McNabb pass with nine seconds left in the game to seal the win for the Patriots?**

a. Rodney Harrison
b. Eugene Wilson
c. Asante Samuel
d. Randall Gay

127. **The win in Super Bowl XXXIX gave the Patriots three Super Bowl wins in four years. Who is the only other team to do that?**

a. Buffalo Bills
b. Miami Dolphins
c. Pittsburgh Steelers
d. Dallas Cowboys

128. **Which actor introduced the Patriots in a prerecorded segment at Super Bowl XXXIX?**

a. Dennis Leary
b. Matt Damon
c. Ben Affleck
d. Michael Chiklis

129. **Who performed at halftime of Super Bowl XXXIX?**

a. Aerosmith
b. U2
c. The Rolling Stones
d. Paul McCartney

2007 SEASON

130. **What was the Patriots record during the 2007 season?**

    a. 16-0
    b. 15-1
    c. 14-2
    d. 13-3

131. **What is the only other team to go undefeated during the regular season?**

    a. Denver Broncos
    b. Miami Dolphins
    c. Pittsburgh Steelers
    d. Baltimore Colts

132. **Three teams came within three points of defeating the Patriots during the regular season. Which of the following did NOT?**

    a. New York Giants
    b. Philadelphia Eagles
    c. Indianapolis Colts
    d. Baltimore Ravens

133. **Who held the Patriots to a season-low 20 points during the regular season?**

    a. San Diego Chargers
    b. Indianapolis Colts
    c. Pittsburgh Steelers
    d. New York Jets

134. **The Patriots broke an NFL record with how many points scored during the 2007 season?**

    a. 558
    b. 565
    c. 589
    d. 619

135. **Which Patriots' player played on the two highest scoring teams in NFL history?**

    a. Donto Stallworth
    b. Randy Moss
    c. Wes Welker
    d. Kyle Brady

136. **Randy Moss set an NFL record with how many touchdown receptions in 2007?**

    a. 21
    b. 23
    c. 24
    d. 26

137. **Tom Brady set an NFL record with how many touchdown passes in 2007?**

    a. 45
    b. 50
    c. 51
    d. 55

138. **Who led the team with 12.5 sacks in 2007?**

    a. Jarvis Green
    b. Adalius Thomas
    c. Mike Vrabel
    d. Rosevelt Colvin

139. **When did the Patriots clinch the 2007 AFC East Championship?**

   a. week 10
   b. week 11
   c. week 12
   d. week 13

140. **How many times was Tom Brady named AFC Offensive Player of the Week during the 2007 season?**

   a. 3
   b. 5
   c. 7
   d. 9

141. **Who defeated the Patriots in Super Bowl XLII?**

   a. Philadelphia Eagles
   b. Seattle Seahawks
   c. Dallas Cowboys
   d. New York Giants

142. **Where was Super Bowl XLII played?**

   a. Dallas, TX
   b. San Antonio, TX
   c. Glendale, AZ
   d. Memphis, TN

143. **What was the score of Super Bowl XLII?**

   a. 17-14
   b. 24-20
   c. 21-10
   d. 28-12

144. **Who was the only Patriot to catch a touchdown pass in Super Bowl XLII?**

   a. Wes Welker
   b. Randy Moss
   c. Donte Stallworth
   d. Heath Evans

145. Who caught the game-winning touchdown pass from Eli Manning?

a. David Tyree
b. Steve Smith
c. Plaxico Burress
d. Amani Toomer

MEMORABLE PLAYERS

146. **Where did Tom Brady play football in college?**

a. Ohio State University
b. University of Michigan
c. Eastern Illinois University
d. University of Southern California

147. **Which quarterback was NOT ahead of Tom Brady on the team's depth chart during his rookie season?**

a. Scott Zolak
b. Drew Bledsoe
c. Michael Bishop
d. John Friesz

148. **When did Tom Brady suffer a knee injury that snapped his streak of 111-consecutive starts and forced him to miss the entire 2008 season?**

a. preseason practice
b. week 1
c. week 2
d. week 3

149. **Who replaced longtime starting quarterback Steve Grogan to start the 1984 season?**

a. Tony Eason
b. Drew Bledsoe
c. Matt Cavanaugh
d. Doug Flutie

150. Where did Marv Cook play collegiate football?

a. University of Iowa
b. Iowa State University
c. University of Northern Iowa
d. Drake University

151. Who became the first NFL player in over 60 years to successfully convert a drop kick when he used it for an extra point in 2005?

a. Tom Brady
b. Adam Vinatieri
c. Josh Miller
d. Doug Flutie

152. What position did quarterback Matt Cassel play in his only career collegiate start at USC?

a. quarterback
b. wide reciever
c. safety
d. tight end

153. What Patriot offensive lineman defeated future WWE and UFC Champion Brock Lesnar in the 1999 NCAA Wrestling Championships?

a. Matt Light
b. Stephen Neal
c. Dan Koppen
d. Logan Mankins

154. Which other former Patriot won an NCAA Wrestling Championship in the heavyweight division?

a. Jim Nance
b. Brian Holloway
c. Pete Brock
d. Lin Dawson

155. Which Patriots' running back moved on to a successful career as an announcer for both ABC and CBS?

a. Tony Collins
b. Keith Byars
c. Craig James
d. Roland James

156. Which Patriots' place kicker played both football and baseball at the University of Memphis?

a. Adam Vinatieri
b. Stephen Gostkowski
c. Matt Bahr
d. Tony Franklin

157. Which former Patriot and NFL Hall of Famer is a 5th-degree black belt in Uechi-Ryu Karate?

a. Mike Haynes
b. Nick Buoniconti
c. Andre Tippett
d. John Hannah

158. Which former Patriot and NFL Hall of Famer earned his law degree while playing in New England?

a. Mike Haynes
b. Nick Buoniconti
c. Andre Tippett
d. John Hannah

159. Which former Patriot and NFL Hall of Famer finished his career with the Los Angeles Raiders?

a. Mike Haynes
b. Nick Buoniconti
c. Andre Tippett
d. John Hannah

160. **Which former Patriot and NFL Hall of Famer played his college football at Alabama?**

   a. Mike Haynes
   b. Nick Buoniconti
   c. Andre Tippett
   d. John Hannah

161. **Where did Patriots' running back Kevin Faulk attend college?**

   a. University of Georgia
   b. Louisiana State University
   c. Florida State University
   d. University of Arkansas

162. **Which Patriot owns a team that competes in the NASCAR Craftsman Truck Series?**

   a. Matt Light
   b. Dan Koppen
   c. Heath Evans
   d. Randy Moss

163. **Which future Patriot became just the second player in NFL history to return both a kickoff and a punt, kick an extra point and a field goal, and make a tackle in a single game when he did it against New England on October 10, 2004?**

   a. Jabar Gaffney
   b. Doug Flutie
   c. Wes Welker
   d. Sammy Morris

164. **Which Patriots wide receiver played minor league baseball with Boston Red Sox pitcher Josh Beckett?**

   a. Wes Welker
   b. Donte Stallworth
   c. Troy Brown
   d. Kelley Washington

165. **Which Patriots defensive player is an accomplished saxophonist who has played with the Boston Pops?**

a. Mike Vrabel
b. Tedy Bruschi
c. Rosevelt Colvin
d. Richard Seymour

166. **Which offensive lineman recovered a fumble for a touchdown in the 2006–07 AFC Championship game?**

a. Logan Mankins
b. Stephen Neal
c. Matt Light
d. Dan Koppen

167. **Which wide receiver took two snaps at quarterback during the Patriots' final preseason game of 2006?**

a. Deion Branch
b. David Givens
c. Troy Brown
d. David Patten

TRANSACTIONS

168. In what round was Tom Brady drafted?

a. first
b. third
c. fifth
d. sixth

169. Who did the Patriots draft with the first pick of the 1971 Draft?

a. John Hannah
b. Mike Haynes
c. Jim Plunkett
d. Sam Cunningham

170. What did the Patriots give the Oakland Raiders in the 2007 trade for Randy Moss?

a. a first-round draft pick
b. a second- and a seventh-round draft pick
c. two second-round draft picks
d. a fourth-round draft pick

171. What did the Patriots trade the Miami Dolphins in the 2007 trade for Wes Welker?

a. a first-round draft pick
b. a second- and a seventh-round draft pick
c. two second-round draft picks
d. a fourth-round draft pick

172. **As of 2009, how many times have the Patriots had the first pick in the Modern NFL Draft (1970–present)?**
   a. 3
   b. 4
   c. 5
   d. 6

173. **Who was NOT a No. 1 overall pick in his respective draft?**
   a. Willie McGinest
   b. Drew Bledsoe
   c. Kenneth Sims
   d. Irving Fryar

174. **To which team was Jim Plunkett traded in 1976?**
   a. San Diego Chargers
   b. San Francisco 49ers
   c. Oakland Raiders
   d. Denver Broncos

175. **Who was NOT selected by the Patriots in the 2008 NFL Draft?**
   a. Jerod Mayo
   b. Terrence Wheatley
   c. Kareem Brown
   d. Bo Ruud

176. **Which school was running back Laurence Maroney drafted out of in 2006?**
   a. University of Wisconsin
   b. University of Minnesota
   c. University of Illinois
   d. Northwestern University

177. **Who did the Patriots select with the seventh pick of the 1996 draft after playing his collegiate career at Ohio State?**

a. Terry Glenn
b. Andy Katzenmoyer
c. Mike Vrabel
d. Tom Tupa

178. **In which round was running back Curtis Martin drafted in 1995?**

a. first
b. second
c. third
d. fourth

179. **Which all-pro linebacker were the Patriots able to lure out of retirement in 2006?**

a. Tedy Bruschi
b. Junior Seau
c. Zach Thomas
d. Ray Lewis

180. **Which team did Adalius Thomas play for before signing with the Patriots as a free agent in 2007?**

a. Miami Dolphins
b. Chicago Bears
c. Carolina Panthers
d. Baltimore Ravens

STATISTICS AND RECORDS

181. **As of 2009, who is the Patriots' all-time leading rusher?**
    a. Curtis Martin
    b. Sam Cunningham
    c. Jim Nance
    d. Tony Collins

182. **Jim Nance is the team's all-time leader in rushing touchdowns with how many?**
    a. 35
    b. 37
    c. 43
    d. 45

183. **Who is the Patriots' all-time leader in receiving touchdowns with 67?**
    a. Ben Coates
    b. Stanley Morgan
    c. Irving Fryar
    d. Gino Cappelletti

184. **Who holds the all-time record for receptions with 557?**
    a. Stanley Morgan
    b. Terry Glenn
    c. Troy Brown
    d. Ben Coates

185. **Who holds the Patriots' record for longest touchdown reception with a 91-yard catch?**

    a. Randy Moss
    b. Wes Welker
    c. Deion Branch
    d. David Patten

186. **Which Patriots' quarterback holds the franchise's all-time record for touchdown passes?**

    a. Drew Bledsoe
    b. Tom Brady
    c. Steve Grogan
    d. Tony Eason

187. **Who holds the team record for games played at quarterback?**

    a. Drew Bledsoe
    b. Tom Brady
    c. Steve Grogan
    d. Tony Eason

188. **Which quarterback is NOT one of the three to average over 200 passing yards per game while with the Patriots?**

    a. Drew Bledsoe
    b. Tom Brady
    c. Jim Plunkett
    d. Hugh Millen

189. **Who is the team's all-time leader in field goals attempted?**

    a. Gino Capelletti
    b. Adam Vinatieri
    c. Matt Bahr
    d. Tony Franklin

190. **Who is the team's all-time leader in field goals made?**

a. Gino Capelletti
b. Adam Vinatieri
c. Matt Bahr
d. Tony Franklin

191. **Who is the franchise's all-time leader in all-purpose yardage?**

a. Irving Fryar
b. Troy Brown
c. Dave Meggett
d. Kevin Faulk

192. **Who set an NFL record with a 108-yard kickoff return in 2007?**

a. Kevin Faulk
b. Ellis Hobbs
c. Troy Brown
d. Tim Dwight

193. **Who is the Patriots' all-time leading punt returner with 2,625 yards?**

a. Dave Meggett
b. Irving Fryar
c. Troy Brown
d. Stanley Morgan

194. **Who is the team's all-time leader in quarterback sacks with 100?**

a. Andre Tippett
b. Willie McGinest
c. Chris Slade
d. Richard Seymour

195. Which Patriot has the most interceptions returned for touchdowns?

a. Raymond Clayborn
b. Asante Samuel
c. Lawyer Milloy
d. Ty Law

196. Who holds the Patriots' record by attempting 691 passes in a single season?

a. Tom Brady
b. Drew Bledsoe
c. Tony Eason
d. Babe Parilli

197. Which running back has twice run for a team-record 14 touchdowns in a single season?

a. Corey Dillon
b. Antowain Smith
c. Curtis Martin
d. Laurence Maroney

198. As of 2009, who holds the team record for receptions in a season with 112?

a. Wes Welker
b. Randy Moss
c. Troy Brown
d. Terry Glenn

199. Which opposing quarterback did Drew Bledsoe combine with to throw for 894 yards on September 4, 1994, which was the second-highest single game mark in NFL history?

a. Warren Moon
b. Steve Young
c. Jim Kelly
d. Dan Marino

200. Who started a team-record 212 games in a Patriots' uniform?

a. Drew Bledsoe
b. Bruce Armstrong
c. Julius Adams
d. John Hannah

ANSWERS

1. c	22. a	43. c	64. b
2. b	23. c	44. d	65. d
3. d	24. b	45. c	66. b
4. a	25. d	46. a	67. c
5. d	26. b	47. d	68. a
6. b	27. c	48. b	69. b
7. c	28. c	49. d	70. d
8. a	29. b	50. c	71. c
9. b	30. d	51. c	72. a
10. d	31. b	52. d	73. d
11. c	32. c	53. c	74. b
12. c	33. a	54. a	75. a
13. b	34. d	55. a	76. d
14. a	35. b	56. c	77. b
15. b	36. c	57. d	78. d
16. c	37. d	58. a	79. a
17. c	38. c	59. c	80. b
18. a	39. a	60. b	81. a
19. d	40. b	61. d	82. d
20. b	41. b	62. b	83. b
21. b	42. a	63. c	84. d

85. a	115. b	145. c	175. c
86. b	116. c	146. b	176. b
87. b	117. a	147. a	177. a
88. a	118. c	148. b	178. c
89. d	119. b	149. a	179. b
90. d	120. d	150. a	180. d
91. b	121. b	151. d	181. b
92. c	122. c	152. d	182. d
93. d	123. a	153. b	183. b
94. b	124. b	154. a	184. c
95. c	125. c	155. c	185. d
96. c	126. a	156. b	186. b
97. c	127. d	157. c	187. c
98. c	128. d	158. b	188. c
99. b	129. d	159. a	189. a
100. a	130. a	160. d	190. b
101. b	131. b	161. b	191. d
102. d	132. c	162. d	192. b
103. c	133. d	163. c	193. c
104. b	134. c	164. d	194. a
105. d	135. b	165. b	195. d
106. b	136. b	166. a	196. b
107. a	137. b	167. c	197. c
108. b	138. c	168. d	198. a
109. c	139. b	169. c	199. d
110. d	140. b	170. d	200. b
111. c	141. d	171. b	
112. b	142. c	172. b	
113. c	143. a	173. a	
114. d	144. b	174. b	